The Beauty In Me

Written By: Elsie Guerrero
Illustrated By: Jerome Vernell Jr.

ELSIE PUBLISHING CO.
WWW.ELSIEGUERRERO.COM

ISBN: 978-1-7327573-7-0

The Beauty in Me

Copyright © 2019 Elsie Guerrero

Illustrated by Jerome Vernell Jr.

For permission requests, write to the publisher at the address below.

Elsie Publishing Co.
Washington, DC
www.elsieguerrero.com
202.670.3282

Dedicatoria

Con mucho agradecimiento, me gustaría dedicar este libro a todos los bells estudiantes con quien yo he trabajado. Por motivos de confidencialidad, no puedo mencionar sus nombres, pero quiero que sepan que han cambiado mi vida y cambiaron mi perspectiva sobre el autismo y trastornos relacionados.

También me gustaría dedicar este libro a mi mentor, la Sra. Dorothy Smith, quien me enseñó que la belleza viene de adentro y que no hay necesidad de decir que eres grande porque el mundo lo verá por sí mismo.

Gracias.

Dedication

I would like to dedicate this book to all the beautiful students I have worked with. Due to confidentiality, I cannot mention their names, but I want them to know that they have changed my life and my perspective on autism and related disorders.

I would also like to dedicate this book to my mentor, Ms. Dorothy Smith, who taught me that beauty comes from within and that there is no need to say you are great because the world will see it on its own.

Thank you.

When you first look at us, you may think we are just like any other kids. We play, we laugh, and we smile. But what makes us unique is that we have autism.

Cuando nos miras por primera vez, puedes pensar que somos como cualquier otro niño. Jugamos, nos reímos y sonreímos. Lo que nos hace únicos es que tenemos autismo.

Having autism doesn't mean we are different. It just means that we are beautiful in our own way.

Tener autismo no significa que somos diferentes. Simplemente significa que somos hermosos a nuestra manera.

Alex may not look up when you call his name,

Alex no mira hacia arriba cuando llamas su nombre,

But Alex is good at making things with play dough.

Pero Alex es bueno al construir cosas con plastilina.

Kevin may laugh out of the blue and make silly noises,

Kevin reír inesperadamente y hacer ruidos,

6

But Kevin is full of joy and loves to play on the trampoline.

Kevin esta lleno de alegría y le encanta saltar sobre el trampolín.

Jenny may not be able to speak clearly as often. She uses gestures to ask for things that she want.

Jenny no puede hablar claramente. Ella usa gestos para pedir las cosas que quiere.

But she follow directions very well and is good at playing basketball.

Pero sige instrucciones muy bien y es buena en el baloncesto.

9

Vanessa may rock back and forth and run around by herself,

Vanessa puede mecerse hacia atrás y hacia adelante y correr sola por todas partes,

But she does it when she gets excited.

Pero ella lo hace cuando esta emociona.

When Flor gets upset, she may throw things and have tantrums.

Cuando Flor esta molesta puede tirar cosas y hacer berrinches.

But Flor is very creative and she has a good memory. Tell her your birthday once and she will never forget it!

Pero Flor es muy creativa y tiene una buena memoria. Dile tu cumpleaños una vez y nunca se le olividara!

Paul has a hard time learning his ABCs and numbers,

Pablo tiene dificultades para aprender el alfabeto y los números,

14

But he loves learning and singing.

Pero le gusta aprender y cantar.

Grace has a hard time saying what she wants, but now she can. She may not be able to have a full conversation, but now she can say what she wants in a full sentence.

Grace tenía dificultades para decir lo que ella quiere. Pero ahora puede. Tal vez no puede tener una conversacion completa, pero, ahora puede decir lo que ella quiere en una frase completa.

"I want chips please!"

"¡Quiero papas fritas por favor!"

Sometimes when Mike gets angry, he might hit himself. It can be hard for him to express his feeling, but he is trying to learn.

A veces, cuando Mike se enoja, puede pegarse a sí mismo. Puede ser difícil para él expresar sus sentimientos, pero trata de aprender.

Mike loves to play with water, just like any other kid.

A Mike le encanta jugar con agua, como cualquier otro niño.

Jenelle has a hard time sharing
and taking turns during playtime.

Jenelle tiene dificultades para
compartir y tomar turnos
durante el recreo.

But her teacher helps her learn how to share her toys and take turns with the computer.

Pero su maestra le ayuda a aprender cómo compartir sus juguetes y tomar turnos con la computadora.

Mrs. Guerrero's

Welcome to our world. We see the world in a different light. But, it is full of love and joy.

Bienvenido a nuestro mundo. Vemos el mundo de forma diferente. Pero, está lleno de luz y alegría.

Kindergarten Class

We are unique and beautiful just the way we are.

Somos únicos y hermosos tal y como somos.